CATHOLIC SUNDAY AND DAILY REFLECTIONS FOR 2024

A Spiritual Companion for Prayer, Worship with Reflections, Readings, and Understanding The Liturgical Year

Jeff Carter

Copyright©2024 Jeff Carter
All right reserved

Copying, altering, or distributing any part of this book without prior consent from the publisher through methods such as duplication, recording, or any electronic or mechanical means is prohibited. However, limited quotations for critical reviews and specific noncommercial purposes allowed by copyright law are exceptions to this restriction.

DEDICATION

In humble reverence and unwavering devotion to the faithful readers who journey alongside me in the sacred paths of prayer, worship, and reflection, I offer this spiritual companion. May it serve as a steadfast guide through the liturgical seasons of 2024, illuminating the richness of our Catholic faith with daily reflections, readings, and insights. With heartfelt gratitude for your companionship on this sacred pilgrimage, may the blessings of the Holy Spirit accompany you on every step of your spiritual journey.

Yours in faith,
[Jeff Carter]

Preface

In the ever-evolving landscape of modern spirituality, the missal stands as a beacon of continuity, a testament to the enduring legacy of the Christian faith. As the author of this book, I am honored to discuss the pivotal role of the missal in nurturing the spiritual lives of the faithful and its profound relevance in their daily sojourn.

The missal, a liturgical book containing all instructions and texts necessary for the celebration of Mass throughout the year, is not merely a functional guide; it is the heart of our communal worship. In its pages lies the rich tapestry of prayers, readings, and rites that have shaped the Christian journey for centuries. It is a sacred repository of divine wisdom, offering solace and strength to those who turn its pages with reverence.

In today's fast-paced world, where the ephemeral often overshadows the eternal, the missal serves as a grounding force, reminding us of the immutable truths of our faith. It is a source of constancy and comfort, providing a rhythm to our days and a framework for our spiritual practices. The missal's relevance transcends the boundaries of time and culture, speaking to the universal human longing for connection with the Divine.

Moreover, the missal is a catalyst for unity, drawing together the faithful from diverse backgrounds into a single body with Christ at the head. Through the shared language of the liturgy, we are invited to participate in the paschal mystery, to immerse ourselves in the life, death, and resurrection of Jesus Christ. This communal aspect of the missal fosters a sense of belonging and identity among believers, reinforcing the communal nature of our faith.

In the daily lives of the faithful, the missal is a wellspring of spiritual nourishment. Its scriptures and prayers are not confined to the walls of the church; they permeate the lives of believers, guiding their actions and shaping their interactions with others. The missal encourages a rhythm of prayer and reflection, prompting the faithful to pause amidst their routines and turn their hearts towards God.

Furthermore, the missal is an instrument of evangelization. In its call to live out the Gospel message, it challenges believers to be beacons of light in a world that often dwells in darkness. The missal inspires acts of charity, kindness, and justice, urging the faithful to embody the love of Christ in their communities.

In conclusion, the missal is an indispensable companion on the spiritual journey, a guide that leads the faithful towards a deeper understanding of their faith and a more profound experience of God's presence in their lives. Its role in modern spirituality is as vital today as it has ever been, for it anchors us in the truth of the Gospel and propels us forward in our mission to live out that truth in the world.

May the missal continue to be a source of inspiration and guidance for all who seek to walk in the footsteps of Christ.

9

Table of content

Introduction to the Missal............................12

Theological Foundations of Liturgy............15

Part I

Morning Prayers and Meditations...............19

Midday Reflections and Examen.................23

Evening Prayers and Compline....................28

Mealtime Blessings: Sharing in God's Bount.32

Special Devotions for Each Day of the Week..34

Part II

The Liturgical Year...37

Advent Reflections: Anticipation and Hope...39

Christmas Reflections: The Incarnation.........41

Ordinary Time: Living the Teachings of Christ..45

Lenten Meditations: A Journey of Repentance and Spiritual Growth..50

Holy Week and Easter: The Passion, Death, and Resurrection of Christ..............56

The Last Supper: The Institution of the Eucharist..............57

Pentecost and Ordinary Time: The Holy Spirit and Living the Gospel..............62

Part III

The Order of Mass..............68

Liturgy of the Word..............73

Liturgy of the Eucharist..............79

Communion Rite..............83

Concluding Rites..............87

Part IV

Sacraments and Rites..............92

Confirmation..............95

Strengthening Commitment to the Church...96

Eucharist..............99

Reconciliation..............104

Confession..............105

The Grace of Reconciliation..............106

Anointing of the Sick..................................109

Holy Orders...112

Matrimony..116

Appendices...122

Index of Scriptural Readings.......................122

40 Uplifting Scriptures for Catholic Faith and Strength...127

Index of Saints and Feast Days...................131

Glossary of Liturgical Terms.......................136

Rites of Blessings and Consecrations...........141

Liturgical Music and Hymns.......................146

Selecting Hymns for Mass...........................149

Guide to Personal and Communal Prayer.....151

- A Message from the Author..............155

Introduction to the Missal

The missal, a cherished vessel of the Church's liturgy, serves a purpose far beyond its physical presence. It is the spiritual compass for the faithful, guiding them through the sacred mysteries of the Mass, the highest form of worship in the Catholic tradition. As a devoted Catholic author, I am humbled to elaborate on the missal's profound significance in worship, personal growth, and community building.

At its core, the missal is the custodian of the Church's prayers, a collection meticulously curated to lead the congregation through the liturgical year. It encompasses the essence of worship, from the Advent's expectant waiting to the joyous resurrection of Easter. The missal is a bridge between the divine and the human, enabling the faithful to partake in the heavenly liturgy.

The significance of the missal in worship cannot be overstated. It is the script of the sacred drama enacted at each Mass, where the faithful are not mere spectators but active participants. Through its pages, the missal invites the congregation to join in the timeless hymn of praise and thanksgiving to God. It is the vessel through which the Word of God is proclaimed, and through which the bread and wine become the Body and Blood of Christ.

The impact of the missal on personal growth is both intimate and transformative. It offers a rhythm to the believer's daily life, with morning prayers that awaken the soul and evening vespers that offer solace at day's end. The missal's scriptures and reflections become a mirror for the soul, prompting introspection, repentance, and a deeper yearning for holiness.

Furthermore, the missal is a cornerstone for community building. It unites the faithful across cultures and languages, creating a universal chorus of Catholic voices lifted in unison. The shared experience of the Mass, facilitated by the missal, fosters a sense of belonging and solidarity among believers. It becomes a source of strength and unity, especially in times of trial and adversity.

NOTE: the missal is not merely a book; it is a living tradition that breathes life into the Church's worship. It is a guide for personal sanctification and a bond that weaves the fabric of the Catholic community. Its pages are a testament to the Church's resilience and adaptability, ensuring that the light of Christ continues to shine brightly in the hearts of the faithful.

In the embrace of the missal, we find the legacy of the past, the fervor of the present, and the hope for the future. May it always remain a beacon of faith, leading us ever closer to the Divine.

Theological Foundations of Liturgy

The liturgy, the public worship of the Church, is deeply rooted in both Scripture and Tradition, forming the backbone of Christian life. It is a rich tapestry woven from the threads of ancient practices, biblical texts, and the ongoing life of the Church. This exploration delves into these roots, highlighting the liturgy's indispensable role in the life of the Church.

Scriptural Foundations

The structure and content of the liturgy are steeped in Scripture. The readings, psalms, and hymns are drawn directly from the Bible, providing a rhythm and narrative that guide the faithful through salvation history. The Eucharistic prayers echo the words of Christ at the Last Supper, as recorded in the Gospels, inviting participants to "do this in memory of me" **(Luke 22:19)**. The liturgy is a living enactment of the Word of God, allowing the faithful to encounter the divine narrative in a tangible way.

Traditions Influence

Tradition serves as the Church's memory, preserving the wisdom of the Apostles and the practices of the early Christian communities. The liturgy has evolved over centuries, shaped by the insights of theologians, the decrees of councils, and the piety of the saints. This living Tradition ensures that the liturgy remains connected to its apostolic origins while adapting to the needs of contemporary believers.

The Liturgy and the Church's Life

The liturgy is not a static ritual; it is the beating heart of the Church's life. It is where the Church expresses its identity, reaffirms its beliefs, and strengthens its bonds of communion. Through the liturgy, the Church fulfills its mission to sanctify the world, making present the redemptive work of Christ. It is a source of grace, a moment of transformation, and a foretaste of the heavenly banquet.

Personal Growth and Communal Identity

For the individual believer, the liturgy is a path to personal growth. It offers a framework for spiritual development, moral reflection, and ethical action. The liturgical cycle provides a rhythm to the Christian life, marking time with seasons of fasting and feasting, penance and celebration.

At the same time, the liturgy builds community. It gathers the diverse members of the Body of Christ into a visible expression of unity. In the liturgy, the faithful stand shoulder to shoulder, regardless of status or station, united in worship and purpose.

In short: the liturgy is a profound expression of the Church's adherence to Scripture and Tradition. It is dynamic, shaping and being shaped by the living Church. The liturgy's roots in Scripture and

Tradition ensure its relevance and vitality, making it an enduring wellspring of spiritual life for the Church and its members. As the Church continues to navigate the challenges of the modern world, the liturgy remains a constant source of strength, guiding the faithful toward their ultimate destiny in Christ.

In the liturgy, we find the essence of the Church's life: a continuous call to holiness, a communal journey of faith, and a sacred encounter with the divine mystery that is both ancient and ever new.

Part I

Daily Devotions

Morning Prayers and Meditations:

As the dawn breaks and the world awakens to a new day, it is a sacred tradition for many to begin with morning prayers and meditations. This time of reflection sets the tone for the day, grounding us in our intentions and focusing our hearts on God's word. The following content is crafted to assist readers in starting their day with purpose and spiritual clarity.

<u>Opening Prayer</u>

Heavenly Father, as the first light of dawn dispels the shadows of night, so may Your grace illuminate my heart. I offer You this day, with all its successes and struggles, joys and sorrows. Guide my thoughts, words, and actions, that I may serve You faithfully and love others generously. Amen.

Scripture Meditation

"Your word is a lamp for my feet, a light on my path." - **Psalm 119:105**

Take a moment to ponder these words from the Psalms. As you prepare for the day ahead, consider how God's word can guide your steps and decisions. Reflect on a passage of Scripture, allowing its truth to resonate within you and direct your path.

Intention Setting

With a calm mind, set your intentions for the day. What virtues do you wish to embody? What goals do you aspire to achieve? Offer these intentions to God, asking for the strength and wisdom to fulfill them in accordance with His will.

Gratitude

Express gratitude for the gift of another day. Acknowledge the blessings in your life, both big and small. Gratefulness opens our hearts to God's presence and aligns our spirit with His abundance.

Intercession

Lift up your loved ones and those in need in prayer. Intercede on their behalf, asking God to provide comfort, healing, and guidance. Remember the wider community and the world, praying for peace, justice, and the spread of the Gospel.

Contemplation

Spend a few moments in silent contemplation. In the stillness, listen for God's voice. Be attentive to the promptings of the Holy Spirit, and carry this sense of divine companionship with you throughout the day.

Concluding Prayer

Lord, as I step into the day before me, I pray for Your presence to be my constant companion. May the meditations of my heart and the words of my lips be pleasing to You. I entrust this day to Your loving care. Amen.

Personal Reflection

End your morning prayers with a personal reflection. Consider the ways in which you can manifest God's love and grace today. How can you be a light to those around you? How can you contribute to the common good?

Incorporating these elements into your morning routine can profoundly impact your spiritual journey. It is a practice that not only enriches your personal faith but also strengthens the fabric of the community of believers. As you move through your day, let the morning meditations be the compass that guides you, the anchor that holds you, and the inspiration that uplifts you.

May your day be filled with the peace and love of Christ, and may your heart be attuned to the whispers of the Holy Spirit. Amen.

Midday Reflections and Examen

As the sun reaches its zenith and the bustle of the morning gives way to the calm of midday, it is a fitting moment for a pause, a time for reflection and examination of conscience. This midday examen is an opportunity to discern God's hand in the unfolding of our daily activities and to realign our hearts with His divine will.

Opening Prayer

Gracious God, as I pause in the midst of this day, I seek Your presence and wisdom. Help me to see the traces of Your hand in the tapestry of my day and to recognize Your voice amidst the many that call for my attention. Amen.

Awareness of God's Presence

Begin by acknowledging God's constant presence in your life. Reflect on the morning past; where did you feel God's presence? Was it in a conversation, a moment of success, or perhaps a challenge? Take a few deep breaths and invite God into this space of reflection.

Review of the Day

Gently review the events of the morning. Recall your interactions, the work you accomplished, and the moments of transition. As you revisit these experiences, ask yourself where you acted in accordance with God's will and where you might have fallen short.

Recognition of Emotions

Identify the emotions that surfaced throughout the morning. Did you experience joy, frustration, peace, or anxiety? Consider what these feelings reveal about your relationship with God and others. How did your emotions guide your actions?

Gratitude

Give thanks for the blessings of the morning, no matter how small. Gratitude opens our hearts to God's grace and fosters a spirit of contentment. It allows us to see the good in every situation and to acknowledge God's generosity.

Seeking Forgiveness

If you recognize moments where you did not live up to your Christian calling, ask for God's forgiveness. This is also a time to forgive others and to let go of any grievances that may be weighing on your heart.

Looking Forward

With the insights gained from this examen, look forward to the rest of the day. Set intentions for how you wish to proceed, asking for God's guidance and strength. How can you be more attentive to God's voice? What changes might you make to better align your actions with your faith?

Concluding Prayer

Lord, thank You for the gift of this midday pause, for the chance to see Your hand in my life and to adjust my path accordingly. As I resume my day, keep my heart attuned to

Your will, and my eyes open to the ways I can serve You and Your people. Amen.

Personal Commitment

End your examen with a personal commitment to carry forward the lessons learned. Resolve to be more present to those around you, to act with kindness and patience, and to seek God's will in all things.

This midday examen is not just a practice but a pilgrimage, a journey into the heart of our day, seeking God's presence and guidance. May it be a source of renewal and a step toward greater conformity to Christ's image. Amen.

Evening Prayers and Compline

As the curtain of night unfurls and the day's bustling activities draw to a close, it is time to gather our thoughts and seek solace in God's protective care. The following evening prayers and compline are designed to offer a reflective end to the day, emphasizing rest in the divine embrace.

Opening Prayer

Lord of the night sky, as the stars take their watch and the world quiets, I come before You in prayer. With a heart full of gratitude for the day's blessings and a soul seeking Your peace, I lay down my burdens at Your feet. Grant me restful sleep under Your vigilant care. Amen.

Thanksgiving

I thank You, O God, for the moments of joy and triumph this day has brought. For the laughter shared, the love expressed, and the beauty witnessed, I am truly grateful. May my heart always be attuned to the countless gifts You bestow upon me.

Reflection on the Day

In the stillness of this evening, I reflect upon the day that has passed. Where have I seen

Your hand guiding me? In what ways have I felt Your presence? Help me to discern Your workings in my life, that I may grow in awareness of Your constant companionship.

Confession and Forgiveness

As night envelops the world, I acknowledge my shortcomings before You, O Lord. Forgive me for the times I have faltered, for the words spoken in haste, and for the opportunities to show Your love that I have missed. Wash away my transgressions, and renew my spirit with Your grace.

Intercession

I lift up to You, Almighty God, those who are in need of Your healing touch, Your comforting presence, and Your guiding light. May those who suffer find solace in Your mercy, and may those who struggle find strength in Your might.

Prayer for Protection

As I prepare to rest, I pray for Your protective care to surround me and my loved ones. Shield us from harm and danger, and let Your angels stand guard over us. In the sanctuary of this night, may we find refuge in Your unending love.

Compline

Into Your hands, O Lord, I commend my spirit. As I close my eyes to the world, may I open the eyes of my heart to You. Let the quiet of this night be a sacred space for encounter with You, and may the peace of Your presence lull me into restful sleep.

Concluding Prayer

God of the twilight, as I end this day in Your care, I rest in the assurance of Your love. May the peace of this compline carry me through the night and into the dawn of a new day filled with Your grace. Amen.

Personal Prayer

In the privacy of my thoughts, I offer You, Lord, my personal prayer. May it be a sweet fragrance to You, a sincere expression of my love and trust in Your providential care.

As we conclude our day, these prayers and compline serve as a gentle reminder of God's unwavering protection and love. May they bring comfort to our hearts and prepare us for the gift of a new day. In the name of the Father, the Son, and the Holy Spirit. Amen.

Mealtime Blessings: Sharing in God's Bounty

Mealtime is a chance to thank God for His gifts and share with others. Here are traditional and contemporary meal blessings:

Before Meals

Traditional Blessing:

"Bless us, O Lord, and these Thy gifts, which we are about to receive from Thy bounty, through Christ our Lord. Amen."

Contemporary Blessing:

"Gracious God, we thank You for providing this food. Bless it as we eat and fill our hearts with gratitude. Through Christ our Lord. Amen."

After Meals

Traditional Blessing:

"We give thanks to You, Almighty God, for all Your blessings. May the souls of the faithful departed, through Your mercy, rest in peace. Amen."

Contemporary Blessing:

"We thank You, Lord, for this meal, the company we shared, and the blessings of the day. Continue to nourish us and guide us in Your love. Amen."

These prayers remind us that every meal is a gift from God, and every moment shared is a glimpse of His love. May they enrich your meals and deepen your connection with God and others.

Special Devotions for Each Day of the Week:

In the journey of faith, each day presents an opportunity to focus on a different aspect of our spiritual life. Here are unique devotions for each day of the week, designed to deepen your relationship with God through trust, service, gratitude, and more.

<u>Sunday:</u> Devotion to the Holy Trinity Begin the week with a prayer to the Holy Trinity, reflecting on the unity and love that flows within God's very being. Meditate on how you can embody that divine love in your relationships.

<u>Monday:</u> Trust in God's Providence Start your workweek by placing your trust in God's providence. Reflect on the Scripture, "Trust in the LORD with all your heart and lean not on your own understanding" **(Proverbs 3:5)**. Pray for the faith to see God's hand in every circumstance.

<u>Tuesday:</u> Service to Others Dedicate this day to serving others in the spirit of Christ, who came "not to be served, but to serve" **(Mark 10:45).** Look for opportunities to help those in need and offer a prayer of commitment to be God's hands and feet in the world.

Wednesday: Midweek Reflection Take time for a midweek examination of conscience. Reflect on the past days and how you have lived out your faith. Ask for God's guidance to correct your path and to grow in virtue.

Thursday: Gratitude for God's Gifts Reflect on the blessings in your life and offer prayers of thanksgiving. "Give thanks to the LORD, for he is good; his love endures forever" **(Psalm 107:1)**. Keep a gratitude journal to record the gifts you notice throughout the day.

Friday: Remembering Christ's Sacrifice On this day, remember Christ's passion and sacrifice. Participate in the Stations of the Cross or spend time in quiet contemplation of Jesus' love for humanity. Offer up any sufferings in union with His.

Saturday: Preparation for Worship Prepare your heart for Sunday worship. Spend time in quiet prayer of confession, and reflect on the readings for the upcoming

Mass. Pray for the Church, the clergy, and for a renewal of faith within the community.

Each devotion is an invitation to draw closer to God and to cultivate a heart that seeks to love and serve Him in all things. May these daily practices enrich your spiritual journey and lead you to a deeper communion with the Divine. Amen.

Part II

The Liturgical Year

Advent Reflections: Anticipation and Hope

As the season of Advent unfolds, the air is filled with a sense of anticipation and hope. It is a time of spiritual preparation as we await the coming of Christ, not only in remembrance of His nativity but also in expectation of His return in glory. These reflections are an invitation to enter into the profound mystery and joy of Advent.

The Season of Anticipation

Advent marks the beginning of the liturgical year, a time when the faithful are called to awaken from their slumber and prepare their hearts for the arrival of the Messiah. The

Scriptures are rich with prophecies and promises of a Savior who will bring peace and justice to a world weary with waiting. In the words of the prophet Isaiah, "The people walking in darkness have seen a great light" **(Isaiah 9:2).** This light is Christ, whose birth we eagerly anticipate.

Hope in the Promise

Hope is the cornerstone of Advent. It is a hope that is not passive but active, a hope that inspires us to live out the Gospel in our daily lives. As we light the candles of the Advent wreath, each flame is a testament to the virtues we are called to embody: hope, love, joy, and peace. These are not abstract concepts but tangible realities that find their fulfillment in Christ.

Preparation through Prayer and Penance

Advent is a time of prayerful reflection and penance. The Church encourages us to use this season as an opportunity for spiritual growth, to make straight the paths for the

Lord. Through fasting, almsgiving, and reconciliation, we cleanse our hearts and make room for the divine guest who seeks to dwell within us.

Joyful Expectation

Despite its penitential nature, Advent is also a season of joy. It is a joy that springs from the assurance of God's faithfulness to His promises. The Gospels recount the joy of Mary and Elizabeth as they anticipate the births of Jesus and John the Baptist. Their joy is contagious, inviting us to share in their exultation.

The Coming of the Light

As the days grow shorter and the nights longer, the symbol of light becomes ever more poignant. Christ is the Light of the World, and His coming dispels the darkness of sin and death. The Advent season culminates in the celebration of Christmas, when the light of Christ shines forth in all its splendor.

In conclusion, Advent is a sacred time of waiting and hoping, of preparing and rejoicing. It is a time to reflect on the profound love of God, who sent His only Son to redeem us. As we journey through these weeks of Advent, may our hearts be filled with anticipation and hope, and may we welcome Christ with open arms when He comes.

May this Advent season be a time of blessing and grace for you and your loved ones, as you prepare the way for the Lord in your hearts and homes. Amen.

Christmas Reflections: The Incarnation

The celebration of Christmas is an invitation to contemplate the profound mystery of the

Incarnation, the moment when the divine became human in the person of Jesus Christ. This event marks a pivotal point in history, where God's eternal Word took on flesh and dwelt among us. The following content seeks to explore and celebrate this wondrous act of love.

The Mystery of the Incarnation

The Incarnation is a cornerstone of Christian faith, encapsulating the depth of God's love for humanity. In the Incarnation, we see the invisible God becoming visible, the Creator joining His creation, the Almighty assuming the vulnerability of a child. This mystery is not merely a historical event but an ongoing reality that continues to shape our understanding of God, ourselves, and the world.

God's Love Made Manifest

In the Incarnation, God's love is made manifest. The birth of Jesus is the ultimate expression of divine love, a love so profound that it crosses the infinite chasm between the divine and the human. The Gospel of John poetically states, "And the Word became flesh and made his dwelling among us" **(John 1:14)**. In Jesus, we encounter God in a personal and intimate way.

The Humility of God

The Incarnation also reveals the humility of God. Jesus was born not in a palace but in a humble stable, not to royalty but to a modest couple from Nazareth. This humility is a model for us, calling us to live lives of service and simplicity, recognizing the dignity of every person, especially the least among us.

A New Relationship with God

Through the Incarnation, humanity is offered a new relationship with God. Jesus, fully God and fully human, becomes the bridge between heaven and earth. In Him, we are invited into a familial relationship with God, becoming adopted children and heirs to the Kingdom. The Incarnation thus transforms our understanding of what it means to be human and what it means to be divine.

The Fulfillment of Prophecy

The birth of Christ fulfills the ancient prophecies and the longings of the Jewish people for a Messiah. It is a fulfillment that not only meets expectations but exceeds them, offering salvation not just to Israel but to all nations. The Incarnation is a testament to God's faithfulness and His plan for the redemption of the world.

The Joy of Christmas

The joy of Christmas is the joy of the Incarnation. It is a joy that transcends the material aspects of the season and touches the very core of our being. It is a joy that comes from knowing that we are loved, that we are valued, and that we have a purpose. The Incarnation assures us that our lives are part of a larger story, a divine narrative that is still unfolding.

In conclusion, the Incarnation is a mystery that invites us to wonder, to worship, and to love. It challenges us to see God in the ordinary, to find the sacred in the mundane, and to live out the implications of the Incarnation in our daily lives. As we celebrate Christmas, let us embrace the fullness of this mystery, allowing it to transform us and inspire us to bring the light of Christ into the world.

May the joy of the Incarnation fill your heart this Christmas season, and may the peace of Christ reign in your life now and always. Amen.

Ordinary Time: Living the Teachings of Christ

In the liturgical calendar, Ordinary Time is far from mundane. It is a period of growth and maturation, where the seeds of faith sown during the high seasons of Advent, Christmas, Lent, and Easter are nurtured. This time invites us to delve deeply into the teachings of Christ and explore their application to our everyday lives.

The Sermon on the Mount: A Blueprint for Living

At the heart of Christ's teachings is the Sermon on the Mount, found in the Gospel of **Matthew (chapters 5-7).** Here, Jesus lays out the principles of the kingdom of heaven, a blueprint for Christian living that challenges us to be salt and light in the world. The Beatitudes, the Lord's Prayer, and the call to love our enemies are just a few of the transformative teachings that, if lived out, can reshape our lives and communities.

The Beatitudes: Attitudes of Being

The Beatitudes **(Matthew 5:3-12)** present attitudes that should characterize Christians: poverty of spirit, mourning, meekness, hunger for righteousness, mercy, purity of heart, peacemaking, and enduring persecution for righteousness' sake. These are not passive qualities but active engagements with the world, reflecting a heart attuned to God's values.

The Lord's Prayer: Our Daily Compass

The Lord's Prayer **(Matthew 6:9-13)** is a daily compass for Christians, orienting us towards God's will and provision. It reminds us of our dependence on God for our "daily bread" and the forgiveness we receive and must extend to others. This prayer is a commitment to live out the reality of God's kingdom here and now.

Love Your Enemies: Radical Love

Perhaps one of the most challenging teachings is the call to love our enemies **(Matthew 5:44)**. This radical love goes beyond human inclination, reflecting the unconditional love of God. It calls us to see the image of God in everyone, even those who oppose us, and to act towards them with compassion and kindness.

The Parables: Stories That Teach

Jesus often taught in parables, simple stories with profound spiritual truths. The Good Samaritan **(Luke 10:25-37)** teaches us to love our neighbor without prejudice. The Prodigal Son **(Luke 15:11-32)** reveals God's boundless mercy. These stories invite us to reflect on our attitudes and actions, encouraging us to embody the kingdom values they portray.

The Great Commandment: Love as the Fulcrum

The Great Commandment to love God with all our heart, soul, and mind, and to love our neighbor as ourselves **(Matthew 22:37-40)** is the fulcrum upon which all other teachings balance. It is a call to a holistic love that encompasses every aspect of our being and reaches out to others in selfless service.

Application to Everyday Life

Applying Christ's teachings to everyday life means seeing every interaction, decision, and thought as an opportunity to manifest God's love. It means forgiving those who wrong us, offering help to those in need, seeking justice for the oppressed, and living with integrity and honesty.

The Fruits of the Spirit: Evidence of Living the Teachings

As we live out Christ's teachings, the fruits of the Spirit **(Galatians 5:22-23)** should become evident in our lives: love, joy, peace, patience, kindness, goodness, faithfulness, gentleness, and self-control. These are not just ideals but tangible evidence of a life transformed by the Gospel.

Note:

Ordinary Time is an extraordinary opportunity to integrate the teachings of Christ into the fabric of our daily existence. It is a time to grow in faith, to deepen our understanding of the Gospel, and to live out the love of Christ in every moment. As we journey through this season, may we be ever mindful of the call to be disciples in the world, living the teachings of Christ with authenticity and grace.

In the ordinariness of our days, let us seek the extraordinary presence of God, allowing His word to guide us, His love to inspire us, and His Spirit to empower us. Amen.

Lenten Meditations: A Journey of Repentance and Spiritual Growth

Lent is a solemn season in the Christian liturgical calendar, observed with fasting, almsgiving, and prayer. It is a time for introspection and penitence, leading up to the celebration of Easter. The following meditations are intended to guide you through this period of spiritual renewal and growth.

Ash Wednesday: A Call to Repentance

As Lent begins with Ash Wednesday, we are reminded of our mortality and invited to repentance. The ashes placed on our foreheads in the shape of a cross are a powerful symbol of our human frailty and God's infinite mercy. Let this day be a wake-up call to turn away from sin and embrace a life of righteousness.

Meditation: Reflect on the areas of your life that are not aligned with God's will. Consider the habits, thoughts, and actions that distance you from divine love. Commit to a Lenten practice that will help you to overcome these obstacles and grow closer to God.

The First Week of Lent: Self-Examination

The first full week of Lent is an opportunity to examine our conscience. It's a time to look inward and acknowledge the ways we have failed to love God and our neighbor.

Meditation: Spend time in silent prayer each day, asking the Holy Spirit to reveal areas of sin or neglect. As you become aware of these, confess them to God and seek His forgiveness. Remember the promise of **1 John 1:9,** "If we confess our sins, He is faithful and just and will forgive us our sins and purify us from all unrighteousness."

The Second Week of Lent: Fasting and Discipline

Fasting is a traditional Lenten discipline that helps us to focus on our spiritual hunger for God. It is a practice that can take many forms, from abstaining from certain foods to limiting distractions like social media or television.

Meditation: Consider what you might fast from this Lent. Choose something that will be a genuine sacrifice, a reminder of your dependence on God. Let your physical hunger or desire remind you to feed on the Word of God and seek His presence.

The Third Week of Lent: Almsgiving and Service

Almsgiving is an act of love that reflects the generosity of God. During Lent, we are called to give of our resources and our time to help those in need.

Meditation: Identify a cause or individual in need and commit to helping them this

Lent. Whether it's through a financial donation, volunteering your time, or offering your talents, let your giving be a reflection of Christ's love.

The Fourth Week of Lent: Patience and Perseverance

As Lent progresses, we may find our initial zeal for spiritual practices waning. This is a time to practice patience and perseverance, trusting in God's grace to sustain us.

Meditation: When you face challenges or feel like giving up, meditate on **Hebrews 12:1-2,** which encourages us to run the race set before us with perseverance, fixing our eyes on Jesus. Ask God for the strength to continue your Lenten commitments.

The Fifth Week of Lent: Suffering and Solidarity

Lent is a time to reflect on the suffering of Christ and to stand in solidarity with those who suffer. It is an invitation to enter into the mystery of the cross.

Meditation: Reflect on the Passion of Christ and the ways in which you are called to take up your own cross. Consider how you can show compassion to those who are suffering and make sacrifices on their behalf.

Holy Week: The Final Journey

Holy Week is the culmination of Lent, a time to walk with Jesus through His final days, from His triumphant entry into Jerusalem to His crucifixion and burial.

Meditation: Participate in the services of Holy Week, immersing yourself in the story of Christ's Passion. Allow yourself to feel the weight of His sacrifice and the breadth of His love for you.

Easter: Resurrection and Renewal

Easter is the joyful celebration of Christ's resurrection and the promise of new life. It is the fulfillment of all that Lent prepares us for.

Meditation: Celebrate the resurrection with joy and gratitude. Reflect on the ways in which you have grown during Lent and how you can carry the lessons learned into the rest of the year.

May these Lenten meditations guide you on a path of repentance and spiritual growth, leading you to a deeper relationship with God and a more meaningful celebration of Easter. Amen.

Holy Week and Easter: The Passion, Death, and Resurrection of Christ

Holy Week and Easter stand at the pinnacle of the Christian liturgical year, commemorating the Passion, Death, and Resurrection of Jesus Christ. These events are not merely historical; they are the foundation of Christian faith, embodying the profound mysteries of suffering, redemption, and eternal life. This narrative seeks to offer insights into their salvific significance.

Palm Sunday: The Triumphal Entry

Holy Week begins with Palm Sunday, marking Jesus' triumphal entry into Jerusalem. Riding on a donkey, Jesus fulfills the prophecy of Zechariah, symbolizing peace rather than conquest. Crowds greet Him with palm branches, a sign of victory, shouting "Hosanna!" Yet, this jubilation is tinged with irony, as the same voices that praise Him will soon cry out for His crucifixion.

The Cleansing of the Temple

Jesus' cleansing of the Temple is a pivotal moment, demonstrating His authority and challenging the religious status quo. He overturns the tables of the money changers and declares the Temple a house of prayer, condemning the commercialization of religion and the exploitation of the faithful.

The Last Supper: The Institution of the Eucharist

On Maundy Thursday, Jesus shares the Last Supper with His disciples, instituting the Eucharist. He breaks bread and shares wine, identifying them with His body and blood, given for the forgiveness of sins. This sacrament becomes the central rite of Christian worship, a perpetual reminder of His sacrifice and presence among His followers.

The Agony in the Garden

After the meal, Jesus retreats to the Garden of Gethsemane to pray. He experiences profound anguish, contemplating the suffering He is about to endure. His prayer,

"Not my will, but yours be done," reflects His submission to the Father's will and His solidarity with human suffering.

The Betrayal and Arrest

Judas Iscariot betrays Jesus with a kiss, leading to His arrest. This act of betrayal by one of His own signifies the depth of human sinfulness that Jesus has come to redeem.

The Trials and Denial

Jesus endures a series of trials before religious and political authorities, facing false accusations and mockery. Peter's denial of Jesus, despite his earlier protestations of loyalty, underscores the frailty of human resolve in the face of fear and pressure.

The Crucifixion: The Ultimate Sacrifice

Good Friday marks the crucifixion of Jesus. Nailed to a cross between two thieves, He suffers the ultimate penalty reserved for criminals. His cry, "**My God, my God, why** have you forsaken me?" echoes the Psalmist's lament, expressing the depth of His desolation. Yet, even in agony, Jesus extends forgiveness to His executioners and assures the repentant thief of paradise.

The Death and Burial

Jesus' death is a moment of cosmic significance. The Temple veil tears, symbolizing the end of the old covenant and the access to God made possible through His sacrifice. His body is laid in a tomb, sealed with a stone, marking the apparent end of His earthly ministry.

The Resurrection: Victory Over Death

Easter Sunday celebrates the Resurrection of Jesus, the cornerstone of Christian faith. The empty tomb, the astonished women, and the incredulous disciples bear witness to the astonishing truth: Jesus has risen from the dead. The Resurrection is the ultimate victory over sin and death, affirming the power of God and the promise of eternal life for all who believe.

The Appearances of the Risen Christ

The risen Christ appears to His followers, offering peace and commissioning them to continue His mission. These encounters transform the disciples from a group paralyzed by fear into bold proclaimers of the Gospel.

The Ascension and Pentecost

The Ascension of Jesus into heaven and the subsequent outpouring of the Holy Spirit at Pentecost empower the early Church to spread the Good News to the ends of the earth. The Spirit's arrival fulfills Jesus' promise to be with His followers always, guiding and strengthening them.

Salvific Significance

The events of Holy Week and Easter are the fulcrum of salvation history. In the Passion and Death of Christ, we see the extent of God's love, willing to endure the cross for our redemption. In the Resurrection, we find hope that transcends the grave, assuring us that in Christ, life is eternal and love is stronger than death.

Note:

The narrative of Christ's Passion, Death, and Resurrection invites us to reflect on the magnitude of His sacrifice and the glory of His victory. It calls us to a life of faith, hope, and love, lived in the light of His Resurrection. As we journey through Holy Week and celebrate Easter, may we be renewed in spirit and committed to living out the transformative power of these sacred mysteries.

In the death and resurrection of Jesus, we find the promise of our own resurrection and the assurance that nothing can separate us from the love of God. Amen.

Pentecost and Ordinary Time: The Holy Spirit and Living the Gospel

Pentecost marks a pivotal moment in the life of the Church—the outpouring of the Holy Spirit upon the apostles, empowering them to preach the Gospel with boldness and fervor. This event, celebrated fifty days after Easter, commemorates the fulfillment of Jesus' promise to send the Advocate, the Holy Spirit, to guide and sustain His followers. Ordinary Time, which follows, is the period in which the Church lives out the implications of Pentecost in the everyday walk of faith.

The Holy Spirit: Empowering the Church

The Holy Spirit's descent at Pentecost transformed a group of frightened disciples into courageous witnesses to Christ's resurrection. The apostles spoke in tongues, a sign of the Spirit's power to transcend cultural and linguistic barriers. The Holy Spirit continues this work today, empowering believers with gifts for ministry, fostering unity, and inspiring the Church to fulfill its mission in the world.

Gifts of the Spirit

The Holy Spirit bestows a variety of gifts upon the faithful, as enumerated by Paul in his letters **(1 Corinthians 12:4-11, Romans 12:6-8)**. These gifts, which include wisdom, knowledge, faith, healing, miracles, prophecy, discernment, speaking in tongues, and interpretation of tongues, are given for the common good, to build up the body of Christ.

Fruits of the Spirit

The presence of the Holy Spirit is also evidenced by the fruits in the lives of believers **(Galatians 5:22-23).** Love, joy, peace, patience, kindness, goodness, faithfulness, gentleness, and self-control are hallmarks of a life led by the Spirit. These virtues are essential for personal sanctification and effective witness.

Unity in Diversity

One of the Holy Spirit's most profound works is the promotion of unity within the Church. Despite diverse backgrounds, cultures, and gifts, the Spirit binds believers together in one body **(Ephesians 4:3-6).** This unity is not uniformity but a harmonious diversity that reflects the multifaceted wisdom of God.

The Call to Live Out the Gospel

Ordinary Time is an opportunity for Christians to live out the implications of Pentecost. It is a call to daily discipleship, to embody the teachings of Jesus in practical ways. The Gospel message is not just to be believed but to be enacted through acts of love, service, and witness.

Discipleship and Mission

Living the Gospel means embracing a life of discipleship, following Jesus' example of humility, service, and obedience to the Father. It also involves participating in the Church's mission to evangelize, to share the good news of salvation with all people.

Social Justice and the Common Good

The Holy Spirit moves the Church to work for social justice and the common good. Inspired by the Spirit, Christians advocate for the marginalized, work to alleviate poverty, fight against injustice, and care for creation. This commitment to justice is a tangible expression of the Gospel's transformative power.

Prayer and Worship

The Holy Spirit draws believers into deeper communion with God through prayer and worship. The Spirit intercedes for us with "groans that words cannot express" **(Romans 8:26)** and guides us into all truth **(John 16:13)**. Worship in Spirit and truth **(John 4:24)** is a foretaste of the heavenly liturgy.

In short, Pentecost and Ordinary Time remind us that the Church is not a static institution but a dynamic, Spirit-filled community called to live out the Gospel. The Holy Spirit is at work, equipping, guiding, and renewing the faithful as they seek to embody Christ's love in the world. As we yield to the Spirit's leading, we become more like Jesus, shining His light in the darkness and extending His kingdom on earth.

In the rhythm of the Church's year, Pentecost and Ordinary Time challenge us to move from celebration to action, from contemplation to engagement. May we be attentive to the Spirit's voice, responsive to His prompting, and faithful in our calling to be Christ's hands and feet in the world. Amen.

Part III

The Order of Mass

Introductory Rites

The Introductory Rites of the Mass hold a special place in Catholic worship, serving as the gateway into the sacred mysteries celebrated in the liturgy. These rites are designed to prepare the congregation for a profound encounter with God and to set the tone for the communal act of worship that is the Mass. Here is an exploration of the significance of each part of the Introductory Rites:

The Entrance

The Mass begins with the Entrance, where the priest and ministers process into the church. This procession symbolizes the pilgrim Church on its journey, and the singing that accompanies it unites the congregation in a common voice, setting a prayerful atmosphere.

The Greeting

Upon reaching the altar, the priest greets the congregation with a liturgical salutation, such as "The Lord be with you." This greeting is not merely a formality but a profound expression of the presence of Christ who gathers the faithful together as one body.

The Penitential Act

The Penitential Act follows, where the community acknowledges its sinfulness and asks for God's mercy. This act of contrition is essential as it prepares the heart for divine encounter, reminding us of our need for God's grace and the forgiveness that He freely offers.

The Kyrie Eleison

The Kyrie Eleison, or "Lord, have mercy," is a short litany that implores God's mercy. Its repetition emphasizes our dependence on God's mercy and the humility required to stand before the Almighty.

The Gloria

On most Sundays and solemnities, the Gloria is sung, a hymn of praise that echoes the song of the angels at Christ's birth. It is a joyful acclamation of God's glory and a proclamation of the Church's faith in the Triune God.

The Collect

The Introductory Rites culminate with the Collect, a prayer that "collects" the prayers of the assembly and presents them to God. The priest invites the congregation to pray, and after a moment of silence, he recites the Collect, which reflects the theme of the day's liturgy.

Each part of the Introductory Rites has a distinct purpose:

The Entrance: helps the faithful transition from the secular to the sacred, from the ordinary to the extraordinary.

The Greeting: establishes a connection between the celebrant and the congregation, rooted in Christ's presence.

The Penitential Act: fosters a spirit of repentance and humility, essential for a worthy participation in the Mass.

The Kyrie Eleison: serves as a plea for mercy, recognizing our human frailty and God's boundless compassion.

The Gloria: lifts the hearts of the faithful in praise, aligning them with the heavenly chorus.

The Collect: focuses the intentions of the worshippers, drawing them into the mystery of God's time.

Together, these rites perform a sacred symphony that attunes the hearts and minds of the faithful to the divine. They form a threshold over which the congregation steps, leaving behind the concerns of the world to enter a time and space where heaven and earth meet. The Introductory Rites are not mere preliminaries; they are integral to the liturgical experience, shaping the disposition of the worshippers and preparing them to hear the Word of God, to offer the Sacrifice of the Mass, and to receive the Holy Eucharist.

In essence, the Introductory Rites serve as a spiritual preparation, a call to worship that is both individual and communal. They remind us that the Mass is a foretaste of the heavenly liturgy and that, through it, we are invited to participate in the eternal worship of the saints and angels. As such, these rites are a profound expression of the Church's identity and mission, encapsulating the journey from sin to grace, from earth to heaven, from humanity to divinity.

In the celebration of the Mass, the Introductory Rites thus play a crucial role in orienting the faithful towards the sacred, fostering a sense of unity and purpose, and preparing them to encounter the living God in the liturgy. They are the first steps on the path to the summit of Christian worship, the Eucharistic sacrifice, where the mystery of faith is proclaimed, and the banquet of the Lamb is shared. Amen.

Liturgy of the Word

The Liturgy of the Word is a central component of the Mass, a time when the community gathers to listen to God's Word proclaimed. It is a dialogue between God and His people, where the Scriptures are read, reflected upon, and integrated into the lives of the faithful. This part of the Mass is not merely a reading of ancient texts but a living encounter with the Word of God, which is "alive and active" **(Hebrews 4:12).**

The Structure of the Liturgy of the Word

The Liturgy of the Word typically consists of the following elements:

First Reading: Usually taken from the Old Testament, it reveals God's workings in history and sets the stage for the Gospel.

Responsorial Psalm: A prayerful response to the first reading, often sung, reflecting the themes presented.

Second Reading: Usually from the New Testament letters, offering early Christian wisdom and exhortation.

Gospel Acclamation: A joyful affirmation of the Gospel's presence, often marked by the singing of "Alleluia."

Gospel Reading: The high point of the Liturgy of the Word, recounting the life and teachings of Jesus.

Homily: A reflection by the priest or deacon, breaking open the Scriptures and applying their lessons to contemporary life.

Profession of Faith: The recitation of the Nicene or Apostles' Creed, affirming the community's shared beliefs.

Prayers of the Faithful: Petitions for the Church, the world, the needy, and the community, expressing trust in God's care.

The Importance of Scripture in the Mass

Scripture is vital in the Mass for several reasons:

Revelation: Scripture reveals God's nature, His plan for salvation, and His will for our lives.

Memory: It keeps the memory of God's actions in history alive, connecting us to the faith of our ancestors.

Formation: Scripture forms us in holiness, teaching us how to live as disciples of Christ.

Guidance: It guides the Church in its mission, offering wisdom and direction for the journey of faith.

Encounter: In the proclaimed Word, we encounter Christ Himself, who speaks to us in the here and now.

Bringing the Readings to Life

To bring the readings to life, one must approach them with an open heart, allowing the Holy Spirit to illuminate their meaning. Here's how the readings might speak to us today:

First Reading: Imagine the struggles and hopes of the Israelites. How do their stories mirror our own journey towards God?

Responsorial Psalm: Engage with the psalm's emotions—joy, sorrow, longing. Let its poetry touch your soul and lift your spirit.

Second Reading: Consider the early Christians' challenges and how the apostolic advice can address our modern concerns.

Gospel Acclamation: Feel the anticipation build as you prepare to hear the words of

Jesus. Let "Alleluia" be a genuine expression of joy.

Gospel Reading: Visualize the scenes of the Gospel. Place yourself within the narrative and listen to what Jesus is saying to you personally.

Homily: Reflect on the homily's message. How can you apply its insights to your life this week?

Profession of Faith: Recite the Creed not as a mere formality but as a personal reaffirmation of your faith journey.

Prayers of the Faithful: Join in the petitions wholeheartedly, aware that you are part of a global community lifting its voice to God.

Conclusion

The Liturgy of the Word is a dynamic and transformative part of the Mass. It is a time when the sacred stories of our faith are not just retold but re-lived within the community of believers. As we listen to the Scriptures, we are invited to enter into a dialogue with God, to be challenged, comforted, and inspired. We are called to be not just hearers of the Word but doers **(James 1:22)**, carrying the message of the Gospel into our daily lives.

In the rhythm of the liturgy, the Word of God becomes the sustenance for our spiritual journey, nourishing us with truth, convicting us with justice, and inspiring us with love. Let us approach the Liturgy of the Word with reverence and expectation, ready to be transformed by the power of the Word and to become its living embodiment in the world. Amen.

Liturgy of the Eucharist

The Liturgy of the Eucharist stands at the heart of the Mass and is revered as the "source and summit" of Christian life. This profound phrase, articulated by the Second

Vatican Council, encapsulates the central place of the Eucharist in the life of the Church and its members. It is in the Eucharist that the Church finds its fullest expression and from which it draws its strength.

The Eucharistic Celebration

The Liturgy of the Eucharist begins with the preparation of the gifts, bread and wine, which are brought to the altar, symbolizing the offering of ourselves to God. The priest then leads the congregation in the Eucharistic Prayer, the Church's great prayer of thanksgiving and sanctification.

During this prayer, the Church believes that the Holy Spirit is called down upon the gifts (epiclesis), and through the words of consecration spoken by the priest, the bread and wine become the Body and Blood of Christ. This change is referred to as transubstantiation, a term that denotes the substance of bread and wine becoming the substance of Christ Himself, even though the appearances of bread and wine remain.

The Communion Rite

Following the Eucharistic Prayer is the Lord's Prayer, the sign of peace, the breaking of the bread (fraction rite), and the Lamb of God prayer, which prepares the faithful to receive Communion. In receiving the Eucharist, Catholics participate in the Paschal Mystery of Christ—His suffering, death, and resurrection. It is a moment of intimate encounter with Jesus, where the faithful are nourished spiritually and brought into deeper communion with Him and with each other.

The Source and Summit

Describing the Eucharist as the "source and summit" of Christian life means that it is both the origin and the goal of all the Church's activities. As the source, the Eucharist is the wellspring of grace and the starting point of our faith journey. It is in the

Eucharist that the Church's mission is initiated, for it is here that Christ's saving work is made present and effective.

As the summit, the Eucharist is the highest point towards which the activity of the Church is directed. It is the ultimate goal of all sacraments and ecclesial ministries. In the Eucharist, the Church is most fully itself, a community gathered around the table of the Lord, celebrating the memorial of His death and resurrection until He comes again.

The Eucharist in Daily Life

The Eucharist also has profound implications for daily life. It calls the faithful to live out the mystery they have celebrated, to become "Eucharistic people" who carry the love and service exemplified by Christ into the world. The Eucharist challenges believers to be agents of unity, peace, and charity, to see Christ in the poor and the suffering, and to work for justice and the common good.

Conclusion

In conclusion, the Liturgy of the Eucharist is not just a ritual to be observed but a mystery to be lived. It is the nourishment for the Christian journey, the pledge of future glory, and the bond of unity within the Church. The Eucharist is a gift of God's love, a call to service, and a promise of eternal life. As the source and summit of Christian life, the Eucharist encapsulates the essence of the Church's mission and the heart of Christian discipleship.

In every celebration of the Eucharist, the Church experiences anew the love of Christ, who gave Himself up for the life of the world. It is a love that compels us to go forth and bear fruit, to live lives worthy of our calling, and to transform the world with the Gospel's message. Amen.

Communion Rite

The Communion Rite within the Mass is a profound moment of unity and grace for the faithful, as they partake in the Body and Blood of Christ. This sacred act is the culmination of the Liturgy of the Eucharist and stands as a testament to the Church's belief in the real presence of Jesus in the sacrament. The rite is not only a personal encounter with the divine but also a communal experience that binds the congregation together in the mystery of faith.

The Essence of Communion

Communion is derived from the Latin 'communio', meaning fellowship or sharing in common. When the faithful receive Communion, they are united not only with Christ but also with each other as the Body of Christ. This unity transcends individual differences, creating a bond of love and peace among all present. It is a unity that reflects the prayer of Jesus that all may be one **(John 17:21)**.

The Grace of the Eucharist

Grace is understood as the free and unmerited favor of God, a participation in the life of God. In the Eucharist, this grace is abundantly bestowed upon the faithful, providing spiritual nourishment and strength. It is a sanctifying grace that heals and transforms, conforming believers more fully to Christ.

Preparation for Communion

The preparation for receiving Communion begins long before the actual moment of reception. It involves a heart open to conversion, a soul cleansed through penance, and a mind attuned to the sacred mysteries. The faithful are called to approach the Eucharist with reverence, recognizing the great gift they are about to receive.

The Act of Receiving

The act of receiving Communion is deeply personal. As the host is placed in the hands or on the tongue, the believer is invited to say 'Amen', a statement of firm belief in the real presence of Christ in the Eucharist. This moment is an intimate encounter with Jesus, where the faithful are invited to commune with their Savior.

The Effects of Communion

The effects of receiving Communion are manifold. It increases one's union with Christ, forgives venial sins, and strengthens against future sin. It also deepens the unity of the Church, as it builds up the Body of Christ. The grace received through Communion is meant to be lived out in daily life, inspiring acts of charity, forgiveness, and service.

Communion as Mission

The Communion Rite is not an end in itself but a sending forth. The Mass concludes with a mission, as the faithful are charged to go out and live the Gospel. The grace received in Communion is to be shared with the world, manifesting the love of Christ in every thought, word, and deed.

The Eucharist in Times of Trial

In times of trial, the Eucharist is a source of comfort and hope. It reminds the faithful of the suffering Christ endured for humanity's salvation and His victory over sin and death. The unity experienced in Communion offers solace and solidarity, as believers support one another in their struggles.

Note: The Communion Rite is a profound expression of the Christian mystery. It is a moment of grace that calls the faithful to unity with Christ and each other. It is a sacred meal that nourishes the soul and empowers the Church to fulfill its mission in the world. As the source and summit of Christian life, the Eucharist is the spiritual food that sustains believers on their journey towards eternal life.

In every celebration of the Eucharist, the Church is renewed and strengthened. The Communion Rite, in particular, is a pledge of future glory, a foretaste of the heavenly banquet, and a reminder of the eternal covenant between God and His people. May all who partake in the Body and Blood of Christ be transformed by His grace and united in His love. Amen.

Concluding Rites

The Concluding Rites of the Mass serve as a bridge between the sacred liturgy and our everyday lives. They are a call to action, a reminder that the grace received at Mass is not meant to be contained within the walls of the church but to be carried into the world. As the faithful are sent forth, they are charged with the mission to live out their faith in tangible ways, to be the hands and feet of Christ in a world in need of His love and truth.

The Dismissal

The Concluding Rites are brief but significant. They begin with any final announcements that pertain to the life of the community, followed by the priest's blessing. The Mass ends with the dismissal, where the deacon or priest exhorts the congregation: "Go forth, the Mass is ended," or similar words. This dismissal is not merely a signal that the service is over; it is a commissioning. The Latin root of the word "Mass" is 'missa', from 'mittere', meaning "to send." Thus, the Mass is a sending forth of the faithful to fulfill God's will.

Living the Eucharist

The Eucharist is the source of the Church's life and mission. It is the spiritual food that sustains us and the bond of communion that unites us. When we receive the Eucharist, we are filled with the life of Christ, and we are called to bring that life to others. The challenge is to live the Eucharist, to make the love, sacrifice, and unity experienced at Mass evident in our daily interactions.

Faith in Action

Living out the message of the Mass means putting faith into action. It means seeing Christ in the poor, the marginalized, the stranger, and the enemy. It means working for justice, offering forgiveness, and practicing charity. It means being a peacemaker, a bearer of hope, and a witness to the Gospel.

The Role of the Laity

The laity has a unique role to play in carrying the message of the Mass into the world. As laypeople engage in various professions and walks of life, they are called to be leaven in the world, to infuse society with the values of the Gospel. Whether in the family, the workplace, the marketplace, or the public square, lay Catholics are called to live their faith with integrity and courage.

The Call to Holiness

The Second Vatican Council emphasized the universal call to holiness, which means that every Christian is called to be a saint. Holiness is not reserved for a few but is the vocation of all the baptized. Living out the message of the Mass means striving for holiness in the ordinary circumstances of life, making every moment an offering to God.

The Witness of Charity

Charity is the hallmark of the Christian life. The love experienced at Mass must translate into love for others, especially the least among us. The faithful are called to be generous in their service, to care for the needy, to visit the sick, to comfort the sorrowful, and to welcome the outcast.

The Power of Prayer

Prayer is the fuel for the Christian mission. The prayers offered at Mass continue in the personal prayer life of the faithful. Christians are called to be people of prayer, to intercede for the world, and to seek God's guidance in all things.

In conclusion, the Concluding Rites of the Mass are a reminder that every Mass is a beginning, not an end. They are an invitation to take the grace, peace, and joy of the Eucharist into the world. As the faithful are sent forth, they go not alone but with Christ, who sends them to be His presence in the world. May all who participate in the Mass be inspired to live out its message with zeal and joy, bringing the light of Christ to every corner of the world. Amen.

Part IV

Sacraments and Rites

Baptism:

Baptism is a sacrament of profound significance in the Christian faith, marking the beginning of a spiritual journey that lasts a lifetime. It is a transformative rite that signifies a person's initiation into the Christian community, embodying the death and resurrection of Christ. Through Baptism, individuals are cleansed of original sin, reborn as children of God, and welcomed into the fellowship of believers.

The Transformative Power of Baptism

Spiritual Rebirth: Baptism represents a spiritual rebirth. Just as Jesus was resurrected, those who are baptized emerge from the waters into a new life of faith. This rebirth is a transformation from an old life of sin to a new life in Christ.

Indelible Mark: Baptism imprints an indelible spiritual mark on the soul, signifying a permanent bond with Christ. This mark is a sign of belonging to the Christian community and a call to live according to the Gospel.

Gift of the Holy Spirit: In Baptism, the Holy Spirit descends upon the baptized, bestowing gifts that will guide and strengthen them on their faith journey. This divine presence is a source of comfort, wisdom, and courage throughout one's life.

The Journey of Faith

Lifelong Conversion: Baptism is the first step in a lifelong process of conversion and sanctification. It calls the faithful to continual growth in virtue, deepening of faith, and active participation in the Church's sacramental life.

Community of Believers: Baptism ushers individuals into the community of believers, the Church. This community provides support, instruction, and fellowship as they grow in their understanding and practice of the faith.

Mission and Service: The grace of Baptism empowers Christians to carry out the mission of the Church. It calls them to serve others, promote justice, and be witnesses to the love of Christ in the world.

In essence, Baptism is a transformative sacrament that sets individuals on a path of spiritual discovery and growth. It is a sacred commitment to follow Christ and a declaration of membership in the universal Church. As the first step in a lifelong journey of faith, Baptism is a celebration of God's grace and the beginning of a profound adventure in the Christian life. Amen.

Confirmation

Confirmation is a sacrament of initiation that deepens the grace received at Baptism and strengthens the individual's commitment to the Church. It is a rite of passage that marks a Christian's mature acceptance of their faith and their role as an active member of the Church community.

The Deepening of Grace

In Confirmation, the grace of Baptism is deepened in several significant ways:

Seal of the Holy Spirit: Confirmation is often referred to as the sacrament of the Holy Spirit. The "seal" of the Holy Spirit, which is received in Confirmation, signifies the indelible mark that identifies the Christian as belonging to Christ. This seal is a spiritual strengthening that fortifies the confirmed in their witness to Christ and His Gospel.

Gifts of the Holy Spirit: The sacrament imparts the gifts of the Holy Spirit, wisdom, understanding, counsel, fortitude, knowledge, piety, and fear of the Lord. These gifts are meant to mature the Christian for the practice of faith and to aid in discerning and carrying out God's will.

Fruits of the Holy Spirit: The confirmed are expected to bear the fruits of the Holy Spirit, which include love, joy, peace, patience, kindness, goodness, faithfulness, gentleness, and self-control. These fruits are signs of a life lived in harmony with the Spirit.

Strengthening Commitment to the Church

Confirmation plays a crucial role in strengthening one's commitment to the Church:

Active Participation: Through Confirmation, the faithful are called to participate more actively in the Church's mission. This participation can take many forms, from involvement in parish life to engagement in social justice issues and evangelization efforts.

Witness to Faith: The confirmed are empowered to be witnesses to their faith, not only in word but also in deed. They are called to share their faith with others and to defend it when necessary.

Unity with the Church: Confirmation strengthens the bond of unity with the Church. The confirmed share more completely in the Church's apostolic nature and are more closely linked to the Church's mission of bringing the Gospel to the world.

The Rite of Confirmation

The rite of Confirmation typically includes the laying on of hands by the bishop, the anointing with chrism, and the words, "Be sealed with the Gift of the Holy Spirit." These elements signify the outpouring of the

Holy Spirit and the confirmed full initiation into the Church.

The Lifelong Journey

Confirmation is not the conclusion of one's faith journey but rather a milestone along the way. It is the beginning of a new phase of deeper relationship with God and more profound participation in the Church. The confirmed are encouraged to continue learning about their faith, to grow in their spiritual life, and to serve the Church and the world.

Conclusion

In conclusion, Confirmation is a sacrament of empowerment and deepening of grace. It marks a significant step in the Christian's journey of faith, equipping them with the spiritual tools necessary for a robust and active faith life. Through Confirmation, the faithful are called to live out their baptismal promises more fully and to embrace their role in the Church's mission to the world. It is a commitment to a life of faith that is ever-growing, dynamic, and responsive to the movement of the Holy Spirit. Amen.

Eucharist

The Eucharist, often called the Blessed Sacrament, stands at the center of the Christian faith as a profound mystery and a source of unending grace. It is the heart of Catholic worship and the summit of Christian life, where believers encounter the real presence of Jesus Christ. The Eucharist is spiritual nourishment that sustains the soul, a call to unity with Christ, and an invitation to live in communion with the Church and one another.

The Eucharist as Spiritual Nourishment

The Eucharist is often referred to as the "bread of life," a term that signifies its role as sustenance for our spiritual journey. Just as physical food provides nourishment for the body, the Eucharist provides nourishment for the soul. In **John 6:35**, Jesus declares, "I am the bread of life. Whoever comes to me will never go hungry, and whoever believes in me will never be thirsty." This statement underscores the Eucharist's role as a source of spiritual sustenance that satisfies our deepest hungers and longings.

In the act of receiving the Eucharist, we are invited to partake in the Paschal Mystery—the passion, death, and resurrection of Jesus. This sacred meal is a reminder of the sacrifice of Christ, who offered His body and blood for the salvation of humanity. The Eucharist is a gift of self from Christ to His Church, a testament to His love and a pledge of eternal life.

The Eucharist as a Call to Unity

The Eucharist is also a powerful call to unity. In **1 Corinthians 10:17**, St. Paul writes, "Because there is one bread, we who are many are one body, for we all partake of the one bread." This passage highlights the communal aspect of the Eucharist. When we gather around the altar to receive Communion, we are united not only with Christ but also with each other as members of His Body, the Church.

This unity is not merely symbolic; it is a real and profound communion that transcends time and space. In the Eucharist, we are joined with the saints and angels in heaven, with Christians throughout the world, and with those who have gone before us marked with the sign of faith. The Eucharist breaks down barriers and fosters a sense of belonging and fellowship among all who believe.

The Eucharist and the Church

The Eucharist is intimately connected to the Church. It is the celebration of the Eucharist that makes the Church. The Second Vatican Council's Dogmatic Constitution on the Church, "Lumen Gentium," states, "The Eucharist is the source and summit of the

Christian life." All the Church's activities and ministries are directed toward the Eucharist, and they all flow from it.

The celebration of the Eucharist is the highest form of worship in the Catholic Church. It is in the liturgy that the Church expresses its faith and receives the grace necessary to live out that faith in the world. The Eucharist is the sacrament of unity, bringing together diverse peoples into one family of faith.

Living the Eucharist

To receive the Eucharist is to accept the call to live a Eucharistic life. This means allowing the grace received in Communion to transform us. It means becoming what we receive—the Body of Christ. As St. Augustine said, "Become what you receive, receive what you are." A Eucharistic life is marked by love, service, and sacrifice. It is a life that seeks to embody the values of the Gospel and to be a sign of Christ's presence in the world.

The Eucharist challenges us to be peacemakers, to care for the poor and marginalized, and to work for justice and peace. It calls us to forgive as we have been forgiven and to love as we have been loved. The Eucharist is a mission to bring the light of Christ to the darkness of the world.

In conclusion, the Eucharist is a profound mystery that lies at the heart of the Christian faith. It is spiritual nourishment that sustains us on our journey, a call to unity with Christ and the Church, and a challenge to live out our faith in action. The Eucharist is a source of grace, a sign of hope, and a promise of eternal life. As we partake of this holy sacrament, may we be transformed into the image of Christ and be united more closely with Him and with each other. Amen.

Reconciliation

The Sacrament of Reconciliation, also known as Confession or Penance, is a profound expression of God's infinite mercy and love. It is a sacrament of healing and a means through which we are reconciled with God and the Church after having strayed through sin. This sacrament allows us to experience the compassionate forgiveness of God and to begin anew with a clean heart.

Understanding Sin and Reconciliation

Sin is a refusal to love, a turning away from God's commandments and love. It damages our relationship with God, with others, and with ourselves. The Sacrament of Reconciliation is the process through which we acknowledge our sins, express our sorrow, and receive God's merciful forgiveness. It restores the grace of God in our lives and reconciles us with the Church, which is wounded by our sins.

The Steps of Reconciliation

The Sacrament of Reconciliation involves several steps:

Examination of Conscience: Before confessing, it is essential to reflect on our actions and attitudes to recognize our sins. This examination of conscience is guided by the Ten Commandments, the teachings of the Church, and the promptings of the Holy Spirit.

Contrition: True contrition is heartfelt sorrow for our sins, accompanied by the intention to sin no more. It arises from a love of God and a desire to be restored to His grace.

Confession

In the sacrament, we verbally confess our sins to a priest. This act of humility and honesty is an acknowledgment of our need for God's mercy.

Absolution The priest, acting in the person of Christ, pronounces the words of absolution, which affect the forgiveness of sins. "I absolve you from your sins in the name of the Father, and of the Son, and of the Holy Spirit."

Penance: The priest assigns an act of penance, which serves as a remedy for the disorder introduced by sin and as a means of making amends. Penance may involve prayer, an offering, works of mercy, service, or sacrifice.

The Grace of Reconciliation

The grace received in Reconciliation is multifaceted:

Forgiveness: The primary grace of the sacrament is the forgiveness of sins. This forgiveness is complete and restores us to God's friendship.

Peace and Serenity: Reconciliation brings peace to the heart, knowing that we are forgiven and loved by God.

Spiritual Strength: The sacrament provides spiritual strength to resist temptation and to live a virtuous life.

Healing: Reconciliation heals the soul, mends our relationship with the Church, and helps to repair the damage sin has caused in our lives.

God's Infinite Mercy

The Sacrament of Reconciliation is a profound encounter with God's infinite mercy. Pope Francis often speaks of the "Church as a field hospital," emphasizing that the sacrament is a place of healing, not judgment. God's mercy is greater than any sin, and He awaits us with open arms whenever we turn back to Him.

Living a Reconciled Life

After receiving the sacrament, we are called to live out the reconciliation we have experienced. This means striving to sin no more, to grow in virtue, and to live in love and service to others. A reconciled life is a witness to the power of God's mercy and a testament to the transformation that His grace can achieve in our hearts.

Conclusion

In conclusion, the Sacrament of Reconciliation is a precious gift that allows us to experience the depth of God's mercy and to be transformed by His love. It is an invitation to turn away from sin and to embrace a life of holiness. Through this sacrament, we are reminded that no matter how far we may stray, God's love is steadfast, and His mercy is without end. Let us approach the Sacrament of Reconciliation with humble hearts, confident in the love and mercy that await us. Amen.

Anointing of the Sick

The Anointing of the Sick is a sacrament of the Catholic Church that offers comfort and healing to those suffering from serious illness or the frailty of old age. It is a profound encounter with God's mercy, a source of strength, and a beacon of hope for eternal life. This sacrament is rooted in the compassionate ministry of Jesus, who healed the sick and cared for the suffering.

The Church's Teachings on Suffering

The Church views suffering not as a punishment or an end in itself but as a participation in the Passion of Christ. Suffering has redemptive value when united with the sufferings of Jesus. The Letter to the Colossians reminds us, "In my flesh, I am filling up what is lacking in the afflictions of Christ on behalf of his body, which is the church" **(Colossians 1:24).** This perspective does not diminish the pain of suffering but offers a way to imbue it with meaning.

The Sacrament of Healing

The Anointing of the Sick is a sacrament of healing. While physical recovery is not guaranteed, the sacrament provides spiritual healing and strength. It is a sign of God's grace that can lead to peace and inner healing, even when physical healing does not occur. The sacrament also offers the forgiveness of sins, if the sick person is unable to receive the sacrament of Reconciliation.

The Rite of Anointing

The rite involves the laying on of hands by the priest, symbolizing the invocation of the Holy Spirit, and the anointing with oil blessed by the bishop. The oil, a symbol of strength, is a sign of the Holy Spirit's presence and the grace that flows from Christ, the physician of souls and bodies.

The Hope of Eternal Life

The Anointing of the Sick points to the hope of eternal life. It reminds the faithful that life on earth is temporary and that suffering is not the final word. The sacrament strengthens the hope of the sick in the promise of resurrection and the life to come. It is a reminder that, in Christ, death is not an end but a doorway to eternal communion with God.

The Community's Role

The sacrament also emphasizes the role of the community in supporting the sick. The prayers and presence of the faithful are a source of comfort and solidarity. The Church teaches that caring for the sick is a corporal work of mercy and a participation in the healing ministry of Jesus.

In conclusion, the Anointing of the Sick is a sacrament that brings comfort and hope to those who are suffering. It is a tangible expression of God's infinite mercy and love, a source of strength in times of weakness, and a reminder of the Christian hope in eternal life. Through this sacrament, the Church continues the healing work of

Christ, offering solace to the afflicted and reminding all of the redemptive power of suffering when united with the sufferings of Christ. Amen.

Holy Orders

Holy Orders is a sacrament of apostolic ministry through which the mission entrusted by Christ to his apostles continues to be exercised in the Church until the end of time. It is, therefore, a sacrament of ecclesial leadership and service. The vocation to Holy Orders is a call to embody the image of Christ, who came not to be served, but to serve.

The Three Degrees of Holy Orders

Holy Orders comprises three degrees: the episcopate, the presbyterate, and the diaconate. Bishops receive the fullness of the sacrament of Holy Orders and are the successors to the apostles. They are responsible for teaching doctrine, governing Catholics in their jurisdiction, sanctifying the world, and representing the Church. Priests are co-workers with their bishops and form a unique sacerdotal community. They are entrusted with the tasks of teaching, leading divine worship, and pastoral governance. Deacons are ordained for tasks of service in the Church; they do not receive the ministerial priesthood but serve the people of God in the ministry of the liturgy, the word, and charity.

The Role of Holy Orders in the Church

Those who receive Holy Orders are dedicated to the service of the Church. They are set apart in the ecclesial community to preach the Gospel, celebrate divine worship, especially the Eucharist from which their ministry derives its strength, and to shepherd the faithful.

The Sacramental Nature of Holy Orders

Holy Orders, like other sacraments, confers grace. The grace of Holy Orders is configured to Christ's priesthood, a grace that enables the exercise of a "sacred power" which can only come from Christ himself through his Church. Ordination imprints an indelible sacramental character; therefore, the sacrament of Holy Orders cannot be repeated or conferred temporarily.

The Call to Holy Orders

The call to Holy Orders is a divine vocation. It is God who calls individuals to serve. The Church discerns the authenticity of this call and confirms it through the rite of ordination. This discernment involves a deep consideration of the candidate's human, spiritual, intellectual, and pastoral abilities.

The Life of Those in Holy Orders

The life of those in Holy Orders is characterized by service to the faithful. They are called to lead a life of celibacy, obedience, and prayer. Celibacy signifies a new way of loving as a total gift to Christ and his Church. Obedience signifies a commitment to the Church's mission, and prayer signifies a relationship with God.

The Mission of Holy Orders

The mission of those in Holy Orders is to build up the body of Christ. They do this by preaching the word of God, administering the sacraments, and shepherding the people entrusted to their care. They are to be models of holiness and dedication, inspiring the faithful to live out their baptismal call to holiness.

Conclusion

In conclusion, the vocation to Holy Orders is a critical and divine calling within the life and mission of the Church. It is a commitment to serve, to lead, to teach, and to sanctify in the name of Christ. Those who receive Holy Orders are entrusted with a sacred duty to guide the faithful on their spiritual journey, to be stewards of the sacraments, and to be shepherds after the heart of Christ. Their role is indispensable in the life of the Church, for through them, the light of the Gospel shines forth, and the grace of the sacraments is bestowed upon God's people. Amen.

Matrimony

The sacrament of Matrimony is a profound manifestation of God's love, a sacred covenant that mirrors the union between Christ and His Church. It is a celebration of mutual commitment, a journey of shared faith, and a testament to the enduring power of love.

The Essence of Matrimony

Matrimony is more than a legal contract; it is a sacramental covenant that binds a couple in a lifelong union of love and fidelity. This covenant is a public declaration of love that echoes the unconditional love God has for humanity. In this sacrament, a man and a woman come together to form a communion of life and love, which is ordained for the well-being of the spouses and the procreation and upbringing of children.

A Sign of God's Love

The love between spouses in Matrimony is a reflection of God's love. It is patient, kind, enduring, and forgiving. It is a love that is not self-seeking but seeks the good of the other. The love in Matrimony is meant to be a living sign of the love that Christ has for His Church—a love that is willing to sacrifice, to give, and to serve.

The Union Between Christ and the Church

Matrimony is a reflection of the mystical union between Christ and the Church. As St. Paul writes in **Ephesians 5:25-27,** "Husbands, love your wives, just as Christ loved the church and gave himself up for her to make her holy." The self-giving love of spouses in Matrimony is a participation in the self-giving love of Christ. It is a love that sanctifies and leads to holiness.

The Sacramental Grace of Matrimony

The sacrament of Matrimony bestows special graces upon the couple. These graces help the spouses to perfect their love, strengthen their unity, and sanctify them on their journey toward eternal life. The grace of Matrimony is a source of strength and guidance, helping couples to navigate the joys and challenges of married life.

The Vows of Matrimony

The vows taken in Matrimony are sacred promises made before God and the community. They are commitments to love and honor each other "for better, for worse, for richer, for poorer, in sickness and in health, until death do us part." These vows are the foundation upon which a strong and lasting marriage is built.

The Celebration of Matrimony

The celebration of Matrimony is a joyous occasion that brings together family, friends, and the faith community. It is a liturgical celebration that includes the exchange of vows, the blessing and exchange of rings, and the nuptial blessing. The Mass, if celebrated, is a sign of the couple's unity with Christ and the Church.

The Witness of Matrimony

Couples who live out the sacrament of Matrimony become witnesses to the love of God. Their marriage becomes a sign of hope and a beacon of light in a world that often questions the value of lasting commitment. The witness of a loving, faithful marriage is a powerful testimony to the presence of God's love in the world.

The Mission of Matrimonial Love

The love in Matrimony is not meant to be kept hidden but is called to be fruitful. It is a mission to bring life, both physically through the procreation of children and spiritually through acts of kindness, service, and love. The matrimonial union is a call to transform the world through the power of love.

Note: The sacrament of Matrimony is a celebration of love, a sign of God's presence, and a reflection of the union between Christ and the Church. It is a sacred covenant that calls spouses to a life of mutual love, sacrifice, and service. Matrimony is a journey of faith that leads to the fullness of life and love in God. May all married couples be blessed with the grace to live out their vows with joy and fidelity, and may their love be a sign of God's love to all they encounter. Amen.

Appendices

Index of Scriptural Readings

Daily Thematic Index

Sunday - The Resurrection

Morning: John 20:1-18

Midday: 1 Corinthians 15:12-20

Evening: Mark 16:1-8

Monday - Creation

Morning: Genesis 1:1-25

Midday: Psalm 104:1-35

Evening: Proverbs 8:22-31

Tuesday - Covenant

Morning: Genesis 9:8-17

Midday: Jeremiah 31:31-34

Evening: Hebrews 8:6-13

Wednesday - Prophecy

Morning: Isaiah 53:1-12

Midday: Daniel 7:13-14

Evening: Revelation 19:11-16

Thursday - The Eucharist

Morning: Exodus 12:1-28

Midday: John 6:35-59

Evening: 1 Corinthians 11:23-26

Friday - The Passion

Morning: Isaiah 52:13-53:12

Midday: Mark 15:1-39

Evening: Psalm 22:1-31

Saturday - Rest and Anticipation

Morning: Genesis 2:1-3

Midday: Hebrews 4:1-11

Evening: Luke 23:50-56

Liturgical Calendar Index

Advent

Week 1: Isaiah 40:1-11

Week 2: Malachi 3:1-4

Week 3: Zephaniah 3:14-20

Week 4: Micah 5:2-5a

Christmas

Nativity: Luke 2:1-20

Holy Family: Matthew 2:13-23

Epiphany: Matthew 2:1-12

Lent

Ash Wednesday: Joel 2:12-18

Week 1: Matthew 4:1-11

Week 2: Mark 8:31-38

Week 3: John 4:5-42

Week 4: John 9:1-41

Week 5: John 11:1-45

Easter

Easter Vigil: Romans 6:3-11

Easter Sunday: John 20:1-9

Easter Week: Luke 24:13-35

Ordinary Time

Week 1: Mark 1:14-20

Week 10: Mark 3:20-35

Week 20: John 6:51-58

Week 30: Mark 10:46-52

Personal Spiritual Goals Index

For Hope

Lamentations 3:22-24

Romans 5:1-5

Hebrews 6:19-20

For Peace

John 14:27

Philippians 4:6-7

Colossians 3:15

For Love

1 Corinthians 13:1-13

1 John 4:7-21

Romans 12:9-21

For Faith

Hebrews 11:1-40

James 2:14-26

Mark 11:22-24

40 Uplifting Scriptures for Catholic Faith and Strength

1. Jeremiah 29:11

2. Philippians 4:13

3. Proverbs 3:5

4. Psalm 23:1

5. Joshua 1:9

6. Matthew 5:9

7. Matthew 18:20

8. Matthew 6:33

9. 1 Peter 5:7

10. John 14:27

11. Philippians 4:6

12. Numbers 6:24-26

13. John 13:34

14. 1 Corinthians 13:13

15. Isaiah 40:31

16. Matthew 11:28

17. Matthew 5:16

18. Matthew 6:34

19. 1 Thessalonians 5:16-18

20. Psalm 34:18

21. Galatians 6:9

22. Psalm 147:3

23. 1 Corinthians 16:14

24. Romans 8:38-39

25. Proverbs 16:3

26. 1 Thessalonians 5:11

27. Psalm 27:1

28. Galatians 5:22-23

29. 2 Corinthians 5:7

30. Romans 8:28

31. John 15:13

32. Psalm 46:10

33. Romans 12:12

34. Ephesians 2:8-9

35. Colossians 3:23-24

36. Psalm 121:1-2

37. James 1:17

38. Romans 15:13

39. Philippians 1:6

40. Psalm 46:1

Index of Saints and Feast Days

St. Peter (Feast Day: June 29)

Originally named Simon, he was a fisherman called by Jesus to be an apostle. He is considered the first Pope and is revered for his leadership in the early Church and his martyrdom in Rome.

St. Paul (Feast Day: June 29)

Once a persecutor of Christians, he experienced a profound conversion and became one of the greatest missionaries and theologians of the Church, authoring many of the New Testament epistles.

St. Mary Magdalene (Feast Day: July 22)

A faithful follower of Jesus, she is celebrated for her witness to Christ's resurrection, being the first to see the risen Lord and announce the good news to the apostles.

St. Augustine of Hippo (Feast Day: August 28)

A theologian and philosopher, he made significant contributions to Christian doctrine, particularly regarding original sin and grace. His works, including "Confessions" and "The City of God," remain influential.

St. Francis of Assisi (Feast Day: October 4)

Known for his love of creation and the poor, he founded the Franciscan Order and is remembered for his simplicity, devotion to poverty, and the stigmata he received.

St. Thomas Aquinas (Feast Day: January 28)

A Dominican friar and theologian, he is renowned for his intellectual contributions to the Church, especially his synthesis of faith and reason in his seminal work, "Summa Theologica."

St. Teresa of Ávila (Feast Day: October 15)

A mystic and reformer of the Carmelite Order, she wrote extensively on the contemplative life, and her works, such as "The Interior Castle," guide many in the spiritual life.

St. Ignatius of Loyola (Feast Day: July 31)

The founder of the Society of Jesus (Jesuits), he developed the Spiritual Exercises, a program of meditation and prayer that has helped countless people deepen their relationship with God.

St. Therese of Lisieux (Feast Day: October 1)

Known as "The Little Flower," she is beloved for her "little way" of spiritual childhood and trust in God's love, as described in her autobiography, "Story of a Soul."

St. John Paul II (Feast Day: October 22)

One of the most influential popes of modern times, he played a pivotal role in the fall of communism in Eastern Europe and significantly shaped the Church's engagement with the modern world.

St. Thomas More (Feast Day: June 22)

An English lawyer and statesman, he is remembered for his opposition to King Henry VIII's separation from the Catholic Church and his martyrdom for upholding the faith.

St. Catherine of Siena (Feast Day: April 29)

A Doctor of the Church, she was instrumental in returning the papacy from Avignon to Rome and is known for her mystical experiences and diplomatic efforts within the Church.

St. Patrick (Feast Day: March 17)

The patron saint of Ireland, he is credited with bringing Christianity to the Irish people and is celebrated for his missionary zeal and the use of the shamrock to explain the Trinity.

This list represents only a fraction of the saints recognized by the Church. Each saint's life and teachings continue to inspire and guide the faithful in their spiritual journeys. The saints' feast days provide opportunities for reflection, celebration, and emulation of their holy lives. Amen.

Glossary of Liturgical Terms

Mass: The central act of worship in the Catholic Church, commemorating the Last Supper of Jesus Christ with his disciples.

Liturgy: The official public prayer of the Church. It includes all forms of worship, not just the Mass.

Liturgy of the Word: The first main part of the Mass, where readings from the Scriptures are proclaimed and reflected upon.

Liturgy of the Eucharist: The second main part of the Mass, where the bread and wine are consecrated and become the Body and Blood of Christ.

Entrance Procession: The beginning of the Mass where the priest, deacon, altar servers, and lectors enter the church or designated place for celebration.

Veneration of the Altar: The act of reverencing the altar with a kiss and sometimes the use of incense, recognizing it as a symbol of Christ.

Penitential Rite: A moment at the start of Mass where the congregation acknowledges their sins and asks for God's mercy.

Gloria: An ancient hymn of praise sung or recited on Sundays (outside of Advent and Lent) and solemn celebrations.

Responsorial Psalm: A psalm sung or recited after the first reading, with the congregation responding with a refrain.

Gospel Acclamation: A short chant expressing praise before the Gospel reading.

Homily: A reflection given by the priest or deacon, connecting the Scripture readings to the lives of the congregation.

Creed: A formal statement of the beliefs of the Church, recited by the congregation during Mass.

General Intercessions: Also known as the Prayer of the Faithful, these are prayers for the Church, the world, and specific needs.

Offertory: The part of the Mass where the bread and wine are presented and the altar is prepared.

Eucharistic Prayer: The central prayer of the Mass, including the consecration of the bread and wine.

Sanctus: A hymn of praise that forms part of the Eucharistic Prayer, beginning with the words "Holy, Holy, Holy".

Transubstantiation: The belief that the bread and wine truly become the Body and Blood of Christ during the consecration.

Communion: The part of the Mass where the faithful receive the Body and Blood of Christ.

Blessed Sacrament: The consecrated bread and wine, which Catholics believe is the Body and Blood of Christ.

Dismissal: The concluding part of the Mass, where the congregation is sent forth to live out the Gospel.

Sacramentary: The book used by the priest, containing prayers for the Mass.

Lectionary: The book containing the Scripture readings for Mass.

Chalice: The cup used to hold the wine which becomes the Blood of Christ.

Paten: The plate used to hold the bread which becomes the Body of Christ.

Tabernacle: The place in the church where the Blessed Sacrament is reserved outside of Mass.

Vestments: The special clothing worn by the clergy during liturgical services.

Liturgical Year: The cycle of seasons and feasts celebrated by the Church, beginning with Advent and concluding with Ordinary Time.

Advent: The season of preparation for Christmas, beginning four Sundays before December 25th.

Christmas: The celebration of the birth of Jesus Christ.

Lent: A season of penance and fasting in preparation for Easter.

Easter: The celebration of the Resurrection of Jesus Christ.

Ordinary Time: The periods of the liturgical year outside of the major seasons, focusing on the life and teachings of Jesus Christ.

Rites of Blessings and Consecrations

In the Catholic Church, blessings and consecrations are special ceremonies where we ask for God's blessings on people, things, or locations. These rituals are very important to the Church because they show how we ask for God's help and favor. Let's take a closer look at different blessings and consecrations, what they mean, and how they should be done properly.

Blessings Blessings are requests for God's kindness and goodness. They come in two types: invocative and constitutive. Invocative blessings ask for God's grace without changing what's being blessed, like when we bless food or people. Constitutive blessings do more than just ask for God's grace; they also set apart a person or object for a special purpose, making it spiritually significant.

Consecrations Consecrations are a type of constitutive blessing that gives something a lasting holy quality. They're mainly for objects or places meant only for religious ceremonies, like altars, chalices, or churches. Once consecrated, these things are reserved for worshiping God and shouldn't be used for ordinary things unless we want to disrespect their sacredness.

Significance of Blessings and Consecrations

Blessings and consecrations are important because they make things holy and set them apart for God's use. They help believers show their faith and commitment, asking for God's presence and safety. These rituals remind us that everything is sacred, including objects and places we use to worship God.

Proper Use of Blessings: Blessings are used in many situations to make moments, gatherings, and everyday items special. For instance, a family might ask for a blessing on their home, praying for it to be filled with love, peace, and safety. Likewise, blessings before meals show thankfulness for the food we have and ask for it to give us strength and keep us healthy.

Proper Use of Consecrations: Consecrations are done by bishops or priests who have the Church's permission. The ceremony usually includes prayers, using special oils, and sometimes incense. For example, when an altar is consecrated, it's anointed with holy oil called chrism, showing it's dedicated to the Mass, where we remember Jesus' sacrifice.

Examples of Blessings and Consecrations

Blessing of a Child: A priest or deacon can bless children, asking for God's protection and grace on them.

Blessing of a Rosary: A rosary can be blessed, making it a special reminder to pray and think about the important parts of our faith.

Consecration of a Church: When a new church is built, it's consecrated, making it a holy place for worship and sacraments.

Consecration of the Chrism: During Holy Week, the bishop blesses the chrism oil used for baptisms, confirmations, and ordinations all year.

Rites of Blessings and Consecrations: The Church's books have details on how to do blessings and consecrations. They include prayers, actions, and sometimes using holy water or oils. These rituals are done with respect and seriousness because they're very important.

In summary, blessings and consecrations are crucial parts of the Church's prayers and ceremonies. They remind us that God is always with us, and everything is special to Him. By taking part in these rituals, Catholics show their commitment to serving God and spreading love in the world.

Liturgical Music and Hymns

In the Catholic Mass, music and hymns are very important. They're not just for worship but also for teaching about our beliefs. Each hymn chosen for Mass matches the time of year and fits with what we read and learn about in the Bible.

Advent: Advent is when we get ready for Jesus to come. The hymns we sing during Advent talk about waiting, hope, and what the prophets in the Old Testament said about Jesus coming. "O Come, O Come, Emmanuel" is a classic Advent hymn that talks about wanting the Messiah to come. It's been around since the 8th century and talks about different names for Jesus that we read about in the Bible.

Christmas: Christmas is a happy time when we celebrate Jesus being born. We often sing songs like "Silent Night" and "Hark! The Herald Angels Sing." "Silent Night" is a peaceful song written in 1818 that talks about the calmness of Jesus' birth. "Hark! The Herald Angels Sing" is a lively song by Charles Wesley that talks about Jesus being born and how it fulfills God's promise.

Lent: Lent is a time when we think about the things we've done wrong and try to make them right. The music during Lent is usually more serious, matching the mood of the season. "Attende Domine" is a chant from the 10th century that asks God for forgiveness. "Were You There" is a spiritual song that makes us imagine we're watching Jesus suffer during the Passion, so we can think about what He went through..

Easter Easter: Easter is the most important time of the year for Catholics because we celebrate Jesus coming back to life. We sing songs like "Jesus Christ is Risen Today" and "Alleluia! Sing to Jesus" to show our happiness and victory. "Jesus Christ is Risen Today" was first written in Latin in the 14th century and later translated to English. It's a powerful reminder of Jesus' resurrection, which is central to our faith. "Alleluia! Sing to Jesus" praises Jesus as our risen King and the one who gives us eternal life, especially through the Eucharist.

Ordinary Time: Ordinary Time is the part of the year when we're not celebrating any big events like Christmas or Easter. The songs we sing during this time talk about Jesus' teachings, miracles, and how the Church grows. "Praise, My Soul, the King of Heaven" is a song that thanks God for his kindness and recognizes Him as our king. "Be Not Afraid" is a newer song that gives us comfort and reminds us to trust in God's plan for us, just like Jesus taught us.

Selecting Hymns for Mass

Choosing hymns for Mass is a careful process that considers the time of year, what we read in the Bible that day, and what we're celebrating. Music leaders and people who plan Masses use resources like the Liturgical Song Suggestions and Liturgical Song Selections to find songs that fit well with what we believe and what we're doing in the Mass.

Theology in Hymns: The songs we sing during Mass have a lot of meaning. They help us understand what the Bible says and what we believe as Christians. For example, songs about the Eucharist, like "Panis Angelicus" or "Tantum Ergo," talk about how Jesus is really with us in the bread and wine. Songs about Mary, like "Immaculate Mary" or "Hail, Holy Queen," remind us about Mary's special role in our faith.

In Conclusion: The music we hear during Mass is more than just background noise. It's a way for us to pray together and learn about our faith. It helps us connect with what we're celebrating in the Church year and teaches us important truths about our religion. Through music, the Church keeps passing on what we believe to new generations, making the songs we sing during Mass a big part of our faith tradition.

Guide to Personal and Communal Prayer

Cultivating a rich prayer life is a deeply personal journey that can also strengthen community bonds. Here's a guide to enhancing your individual and communal prayer experiences:

Personal Prayer

1. Make Prayer a Habit: Choose a specific time each day for prayer to keep a steady rhythm in your spiritual life. Whether it's in the morning, evening, or during breaks, sticking to a routine is important.

2. Set Up a Quiet Place: Find a peaceful spot in your home where you won't be disturbed for prayer. It could be a simple corner with a chair and a table or include religious symbols that inspire you.

3. Try Different Ways to Pray: Don't stick to just one type of prayer. Explore silent meditation, reading spiritual texts, or writing your thoughts to God. Trying different methods can keep your prayer life interesting.

4. Be Honest in Prayer: Share your true feelings with God – your joys, sorrows, fears, and hopes. Being authentic in prayer helps you grow closer to the divine.

5. Stay Present in Prayer: Focus fully on your prayer time. If your mind wanders, gently bring it back to your intentions. Being mindful improves the quality of your prayer.

6. Read and Reflect: Spend time regularly reading and thinking about spiritual writings. This can give you new insights and deepen your understanding of your faith.

Community Prayer

Attend Community Worship: Join in services at your place of worship. Being part of a praying community can uplift you and help you feel connected.

Join Prayer Groups: Get involved in small groups that meet for prayer. These groups offer support and a chance to share your thoughts with others.

Volunteer for Prayer Ministries: Many communities have groups that pray for those in need. This can be a meaningful way to connect with others and make a difference.

Arrange Retreats: Retreats offer a chance for deeper reflection and connection. They can be a source of spiritual renewal for everyone involved.

Take Part in Festivals: Participate in religious celebrations and traditions. These events often involve prayer and are opportunities for community bonding.

Include Youth: Encourage young people to join in prayer activities. This can help them develop a lifelong habit of prayer and keep the community's spiritual life vibrant.

A Message from the Author

As the one who made this prayer book, I've been thinking about how I got here. It's been a journey filled with faith and learning. My idea for making this prayer book came from my strong belief in God, which grew over many years of thinking and praying. The Catholic traditions I grew up with also inspired me.

Since I was little, the different times in the Church calendar have always been important to me. Waiting for Christmas during Advent, celebrating Christmas, being sorry during Lent, and the happiness of Easter, each season taught me something special. But it was in my quiet times of daily prayer, like before sunrise or at night, that I felt like I should make something to help others on their spiritual journey.

This prayer book is the result of that feeling. It's a work of love, filled with passages from the Bible, traditions of the Church, and my own thoughts. I hope it's more than just a book of prayers and readings; I want it to be like a light for people who need comfort, guidance, and a stronger connection to their faith. Through this prayer book, I want to connect the old ways of the Church with the new ways, and bring together the Church as a whole with each person's soul.

When I made this prayer book, I looked to what the Church teaches, the wisdom of holy people, and the experiences of believers. Each part of the book was chosen carefully and with prayer, to help people grow in their faith. Whether you use it alone or with others, my hope is that this prayer book will make your relationship with God stronger, by showing you the wisdom of the Bible and the traditions of the Church.

In Catholic worship: the prayer book is like a thread that connects our personal prayers with the prayers we say together as a community. As someone who deeply believes in the Church's traditions, I see the prayer book as a guide for people's personal prayers. It helps us pray every day in a structured way, following the Church's teachings through readings from the Bible and prayers.

In our community: the prayer book is like the music we all sing together. It helps us follow the order of the Mass and makes sure we all pray together as one when we celebrate the Eucharist. The prayer book is like the script for our faith, helping us act out the story of God's love together. It's in this double role that the prayer book really matters, helping us grow closer to God on our own and as a community, through our shared prayers and rituals.

Remember, a strong prayer life comes from regular practice and openness to new experiences, both alone and with others. By nurturing your personal prayer and participating in communal prayer, you can feel the profound benefits of connecting with the divine.

Made in the USA
Las Vegas, NV
09 June 2024

90921192R00089